What are my chances?

Life Management Explained

WHAT ARE MY CHANCES?

Life Management Explained

Vicente "Tex" S. Hernandez

Polaris Publishing

Manila, 2026

© 2026 Vicente Javier Stabile Hernandez
All rights reserved.

First Edition April 3, 2025

Second Edition

No part of this publication may be reproduced, duplicated, or transmitted in any form—electronic or printed—without prior written permission from the author. Recording of this work is strictly prohibited.

The cover features the Greek Wheel of Fortune alongside a statue of Tyche, the goddess of fortune and chance.

Image Credits.

Unless otherwise indicated, the images in this book were created using AI-assisted rendering tools, guided by the author's conceptual and compositional direction. These visuals serve as symbolic companions to the text, reflecting its philosophical and emotional themes.

This title—alongside blog articles on related topics and upcoming additions to the series—can be found at echoepolaris.com, echoesofpolaris.com, or by searching on Google Play Books or Amazon Kindle.

Distributed by Amazon Kindle.

He deals the cards to find the answer
The sacred geometry of chance
The hidden law of a probable outcome
The numbers lead a dance

Miller and Sting, *The Shape of My Heart*

CONTENT

CONTENT vii
Introduction 1
Chapter One: Meaning 5
    Chances, Choices, and Options 9
    Elemental Values 12
    Realignments 16
Chapter Two: Management 21
    Blueprints of Human Achievements 24
    A Case for Managing Your Life 27
    The Importance of Planning 31
Chapter Three: Essentials 35
    Personal Development Literature 38
    Why Life Management Matters 44
Chapter Four: Context 49
    Relationship and Family 52
    Relevance 53
    Value-Driven Life Management 56
    The Importance of Keeping a Diary 59
Chapter Five: Assessment 63

  Lucrative Employment 63
  Personal Financial Planning 66
Chapter Six: Security 73
  Building a Great Financial Future 73
  Investment 76
  Popular Budgeting Methods 77
Chapter Seven: Capacity 83
  What Are You Good At? 85
  Competency 89
  Self-Assessment 94
Conclusion 99
Appendix 103
About the Author 107
Other Works by the Author 109
Notes 111

Introduction

He deals the cards as a meditation
And those he plays never suspect
He doesn't play for the money he wins
He doesn't play for respect

He deals the cards to find the answer
The sacred geometry of chance
The hidden law of a probable outcome
The numbers lead a dance

I know that the spades are the swords of a soldier
I know that the clubs are weapons of war
I know that diamonds mean money for this art
But that's not the shape of my heart

Sting and Dominic Miller wrote this song for their 1993 album, *Ten Summoner's Tales*. Sting said that "Dom came in with this fantastic riff — beautiful cadence, sort of Bach-like descending bassline. So, we spent the morning structuring it, making it into a song... A few hours later I've got at least the concept of what the song is telling me... It just occurs to me, but the music tells me the story."

Sting explained that through *The Shape of My Heart*, he wanted to tell the story of a "Card player, a gambler who gambles not to win but to try to figure out something; to figure out some kind of mystical logic in luck, or chance; some kind of scientific, almost religious law." [1] The lyrics prompt us to scrutinize the gambler's mindset while gradually building anticipation for how the story will end.

The song's poetic charge compels me to reflect on my choices. This is deeply personal, and no one realizes what my true intentions are. I am searching for answers that may lie hidden among the odds. Yet, *diamonds*, *clubs*, and *swords* don't feel right; they don't align with the shape of my heart.

The recurring coda—'that's not the shape of my heart'—resonates throughout the song, inspiring moments of introspection. It challenges me to be honest about what lies within my heart.

The song's bridge is remarkable for the change in the tone and the clarity that it gives to the questions posed before.

If I told you that I loved you
You'd maybe think there's something wrong
I'm not a man of too many faces
The mask I wear is one

But those who speak know nothing
And find out to their cost
Like those who curse their luck in too many places
And those who fear are lost

All of a sudden, the singer's genuine emotions come to light. In expressing his feelings, the true shape of the protagonist's heart is revealed.

His choice is driven by love. He is determined to prove that his love is real, despite what others might claim. They know nothing about this matter as they are, in some way, misled.

Sting's masterpiece spurs me to reflect on my choices. My heart is shaped by the decisions I make, and the options before me give meaning to my life.

Many believe that a winning slot machine spin, a roulette bet, a bingo pattern, a pass line in dice, or a blackjack hand is driven more by chance than by skill. Can we compare life's alternatives to a game of chance? Are our choices shaped by luck—or, to some extent, by a destiny that defies reason?

This short preamble invites us into a world where choices and meaning are essential, both shaping the contours and the future of our lives.

Chapter One: Meaning

Life had no meaning for those living in the concentration camp—as narrated by Viktor Frankl—and they looked for means to end it. Just to visualize what Viktor described is dreadful.

In his Auschwitz's recount, the Jews had no rights and could expect only brutality from the Nazi captors. The living conditions were extreme. They endured hard labor in cold, hunger, and exhaustion with minimal food and rest.

Fig. 1: Air-Quad UG. Auschwitz-Birkenau State Museum.
(CC BY-SA 3.0 DE via Wikimedia Commons).

"We were unable to clean our teeth, and yet, in spite of that and a severe vitamin deficiency, we had healthier gums than ever before. We had to wear the same shirts for half a year, until they had lost all appearance of being shirts. For days we were unable to wash, even partially, because of frozen water-pipes, and yet the sores and abrasions on hands which were dirty from work in the soil did not suppurate (that is, unless there was frostbite)."

Prisoners were subject to beating, public shaming, and psychological torture. "The thought of suicide was entertained by nearly everyone, if only for a brief time. It was born of the hopelessness of the situation, the constant danger of death looming over us daily and hourly, and the closeness of the deaths suffered by many of the others."[2]

What could have motivated them to live? They have been deprived of every hope. A return to a normal life, to their families, had completely disappeared from their horizons. Only a strong-minded person could react and manage the pressure, but few kept their wits. The collapse of their psyche went from shock to apathy and depersonalization. The useless effort to comprehend their situation gave way to emotional numbness, ending in the complete loss of identity.

Their testimonies reveal that a life stripped of humanity, especially in the psychological sense, inevitably leads to collapse. There is something precious in life that continually drives us forward. We discover that it's not just a desire to survive but also a deep longing to create and give life. The power of life within us is expressed in many forms, not just physically. Our lives touch others in meaningful ways.

Life only begins to lose its meaning when we fail to honor its true power.

Viktor Frankl spent three years in various Nazi concentration camps, including Theresienstadt, Auschwitz, and Dachau. As a survivor, he shared with the others a sense of purpose that would shape his life work. The key was to find meaning and as a doctor he was often called to help those who wanted to give up.

Fig. 2: Auschwitz-Birkenau Selection Ramp
(Bernhard Walter. Public Domain.
The Daily Beast via Wikimedia Commons)

What could fill up their emptiness? Viktor gave them purpose in their struggle to survive. Some prisoners found meaning in a sense of solidarity and compassion for the rest. Others kept going to preserve a sense of dignity and survive to speak of their ordeal. Most found strength in the love of someone and in the hope for a better future; hell was not here to stay. Imagination played its role too, often bringing solace in the company of wife, family, friends, or projects.

8—Meaning

Frankl's experiences led him to the development of his own form of psychotherapy. Logotherapy's approach is grounded on the belief that the primary human drive is the search for meaning in life. We are not 'predetermined,' no matter what the latest genome theory dictates. We act freely, even in the midst of suffering and deprivation, through motivation.

Fig. 3: Logotherapy Key Principles
(Viktor Frankl)

Logotherapy's key principles connect freedom, will, and meaning in a dynamic interplay of significance. The first principle, 'Freedom of Will,' highlights the autonomy and control we possess beyond the purely physical and psychological, regardless of the odds we face. The second principle, 'Will to Meaning,' emphasizes the power that we have to shape our own destiny. Finally, the third principle, 'Meaning of Life,' explores our capacity to make the best of each situation by identifying and embracing its meaning.

Chances, Choices, and Options

Society today does not resemble a concentration camp, but we still need meaning. What is it that gives meaning to my life? What does direction in my life entail? How do I chart a course toward personal achievements? Or in other words, what infuses my life with meaning? How do I guide myself toward goals that are worth pursuing?

Knowing what to place in a life project is as important as the stages we take to achieve it. Our choices not only define us but also unlock new possibilities, shaping our lives, influencing our communication, expanding our horizons.

Chances and choices seem to be intimately interlinked. Both are conduits of meaning, but not of fate: we will always have an option, even when our choices—often shaped by chance—are limited.

Here, we speak of chances primarily as opportunities. We understand choices as the range of possibilities offered to us. We distinguish them from options, which are our attitudes toward those opportunities.

Let's illustrate this with an example. Many people today are drawn to computer programming, learning a language and designing applications for personal or commercial use.

10—Meaning

Here, knowledge of the language and the logic of the code are essential. We may have written pages and pages of code that lead us to a dead end—apparently without a choice and with no chance of recovering the time spent writing it.

Yet even in such a stalemate, two options remain: one excruciating, the other radical. The excruciating option is to keep studying the language or seek help from other programmers in online forums. The radical option is to scrap the entire codebase and start again from the beginning.

Fig. 4: A painter might dislike his latest work and decide to erase part of it or start again

Similarity, a painter might dislike his latest work—realizing that it does not truly express the right feelings or meet expectations—and decide to erase part of it or start again.

A fiction writer, after producing pages and pages of characterization, may reach a point of no return when he realizes that his novel is losing meaning because the protagonists no longer fit the plot. Again, he may have the option to reflect on how best to introduce the leading characters—which would force him to rewrite everything—or to remove the problematic parts of his novel.

Every one of us, in a way, engages in creative or artistic work that confronts us with similar problems. We select a course of action that leads to a dead end, and so we are forced to consider redirecting our efforts toward a different objective or starting again from the beginning. Every new alternative compels us to evaluate new choices, directs us toward new challenges, and the process repeats itself.

However, options are not cost-free; the path we choose may lead us closer to our objective or drive us farther away from it. Eventually, each of us must scrutinize his or her options, either to correct a course or to start again from scratch.

We need to strengthen that sense of propriety that allows us to recognize and distinguish the good from the bad; we need to cultivate our ethical character.

"Ethics helps us discover what is good in order to follow it and what is bad in order to avoid it. Moral or ethical character enables us to make morally sound decisions and act ethically in life. Ethical behavior focuses on understanding and following ethical values. If our ethical values are poor, our decisions might lead us to waste not only our talents but even our opportunities."[3]

Elemental Values

What is the deepest reason for living ethically? Which down-to-earth value can truly give meaning to our lives? Is happiness really the goal we all pursue, or only the one we most often name? And if happiness is what we seek, where do we begin to look for it?

Our choices often stem from an inner drive that's deeply tied to what we genuinely care about and love. It's like an internal compass—guiding us toward decisions that reflect our true passions and values, regardless of external circumstances or challenges.

This fundamental value we all seek—often in others, and just as often misplaced in the excesses of our own self-regard—is love. Love is the value beneath every other value, the one that gives meaning, proportion, and direction to everything else.

"Man cannot live without love. The need to love is essential and is inscribed in his heart. It is the first natural impulse…[however,] all true love must lead to personal progress. It is clear that this is not easy."[4]

That deep desire for love is sung again and again by singers all over the world. Love songs have been a dominant theme in music across various genres and cultures for centuries. "According to a study conducted in 2024, approximately 60% of all songs release in a given year are about love."[5] From folk music to modern hits, passing through genders like R&R, rock, blues… love songs have dominated the music industry forever. Why this? The singers look for inspiration in real-life experiences which evoke strong emotions. Emotional resonance makes songs popular; love is universal. Love songs bring people together, creating connections. It is the preferred language of communication to express exclusivity, devotion, and passion.

Fig. 5: What is love? (Freepik)

However, love is the desire for what is good for the other person not just a selfish desire contained and nurtured within us. "Properly understood, and in the most immediate sense, love is only love to the extent that it concerns another person... Happiness is love's outcome, never its motive."[6]

"The basic anthropological point is that the human person is not self-sufficient, but needs others... Each human person, in the awareness of his or her contingency, wishes to be loved: to be in some way unique for someone. Each one, if he or she does not find anyone to love him or her, is haunted by the temptation to feel worthless."[7]

Life gains meaning on the pursuit of love. Life can turn into something beautiful through love, but a love outside us. We truly love someone for what he or she is, not for the benefit that we draw from him or her. (Here, we can understand the nature of love for a physically or mentally ill person who is indifferent to us.)

A true love will bring anyone to love without expecting anything in return. This outpouring of love can be meaningful even in the simplicity of doing something good for others because we find reciprocity in the act.

The feeling of selfish reciprocity is fleeting; however, any act done for the sake of others is truly meaningful. Genuine love and selflessness create a lasting impact, enriching both the giver and the receiver.[8]

Self-love cannot keep up to the demand. Our ego cannot love back; we are just one, not two people. If my goals revolve solely around myself, ignoring the broader purpose of living for others, achieving my objectives becomes meaningless, disappointing.

Love Your Body is a song by French singer Amanda Lear released in 1983 by Ariola Records. Jennifer Lopez has been promoting body positivity and self-love for many years, but her use of the expression 'Love Your Body' gained more prominence around 2015. She has often spoken about embracing her body and encouraging others to do the same, especially in the face of body-shaming and unrealistic beauty standards in Hollywood.[9]

Fig. 6: Our ego cannot love back.

'Love yourself' and 'Love your body' have altruistic components. However, the endless dissatisfaction of self-directed, self-contain desires and acts is an experience that we can all relate to. The end of it is a lonely life. Some people might say, 'I prefer a lone life rather that a stressful one with people to care for.' The true outcome of people who think in those terms is reflected in the statistics provided by the networks.

Studies on the matter reveal that "Loneliness causes people to feel empty, alone, and unwanted. People who are lonely often crave human contact, but their state of mind makes it more difficult to form connections with others... the risk of premature death due to loneliness increased by 26% and 29% due to social isolation. Furthermore, the lack of social connection can increase the risk of anxiety, depression, stroke, heart disease, and dementia."[10]

The desire for love is only satisfying outside oneself. This is part of our human nature. To fight it equates to going crazy. Love, the life-giving power within us, has the potential to turn everything we do into something meaningful. But finding meaning in love implies keeping the meaning of love: love will always need nurturing.

"To commit to loving someone is making space for his or her emotional life. There is no authentic love if there is no voluntary commitment through which one takes charge of caring for and attending to the person loved... Commitment, responsibility, loyalty; this is the progression that leads to happiness."[11]

We keep love alive through care and fondness. Love is in the small details, in the showing of affection, and the willingness to sacrifice for love.

Realignments

Ultimately, we all want a life. What this life means for each one of us is a matter of personal reflection. Perhaps you already know what you want, you might even have a plan, but are your plans truly aligned? Are you managing your life towards meaning? State your priorities. Stage your plans. Start right. Choose meaningfully.

Scrutinize every chance offered to you; not every card in a poker game is a winner. Some opportunities look promising at first glance but collapse under closer inspection. Others seem insignificant yet hold the potential to change everything. What matters is learning to tell the difference before you place your bet.

Fig. 7: Not every card in a poker game is a winner (*Freepik*).

We need to examine the values we live by. Guided by the themes of this chapter, let us look at what life offers through the lens of our most basic and meaningful value: love.

Prioritizing materialistic values is nothing new in modern society. In ancient Greek tradition, human ambitions were embodied in the powers and responsibilities of the twelve Olympian gods who resided on Mount Olympus.

Zeus (sky), Poseidon (sea), Hades (underworld), and Ares (war) governed the world, the living, and the dead with their immense power. Artemis (hunting), Demeter (agriculture), Hephaestus (metallurgy), and Hermes (trade) brought wealth through the most prosperous occupations of their time. Meanwhile, Hera (marriage), Athena (wisdom), Apollo (arts), and Aphrodite (love) inspired the deepest and most enriching human values.

Fig. 8: Twelve were the Olympian gods who resided on Mount Olympus.

Though named differently in other cultures, these divine figures symbolize universal human pursuits. Across cultures, *power*, *wealth*, and *pleasure* have been revered as the ultimate goals and the pinnacle of happiness and fulfillment.

Clearly, not much has changed. People today still chase the same desires. However, we have the power to shift their focus, realigning them with what truly matters.

Why not approach it differently? I want *wealth*—not just for myself, but for my family, my friends, my business partners, and those who rely on me. The same could be said for *power*: in my position, I aim to improve services, enhance the environment, exert a positive influence, and make a meaningful difference. And what about pleasure? True pleasure lies in marriage, in love, in mastering a craft, in acquiring skills, in fostering peace, and in creating a nurturing environment for my family.

We conclude this chapter with the desire to set priorities right and design a plan based on meaningful goals.

Chapter Two: Management

Homo sapiens were anatomically similar to us. Our oldest known ancestor was discovered in 1960 at Jebel Irhoud, Morocco, during a mining operation that accidentally uncovered fossilized human remains. Initially thought to be just a mere 40,000 years old, newer dating methods have given these remains a much more impressive, and frankly surprising, age of 300,000 years.[12]

Fig. 9: AI rendering of the *Homo sapiens* as found at Jebel Irhoud in Morocco.

Archaeologists working at Jebel Irhoud in Morocco uncovered not only early Homo sapiens remains but also a suite of artifacts that illuminate how these ancient populations lived. The mix of modern human anatomy, sophisticated stone tools, evidence of fire use, and organized subsistence strategies suggests that key aspects of human behavior and biology were taking shape far earlier than once believed, and across the African continent rather than confined to the East. These findings are forcing researchers to rewrite the opening chapters of our prehistory.

Despite these discoveries, much about the lifestyle of early *Homo sapiens* remains a mystery. However, more recent findings, such as the Lake Mungo man and woman from around 40,000 years ago in New South Wales, shed light on cremation practices and the existence of a vibrant community life.[13]

Fig. 10: Cro-Magnons, 40,000 years ago.

What where the challenges in the life of the *Homo sapiens*? Most likely, his life wasn't very different from ours (hard to believe, right?), though the environment he lived in made his circumstances unique by modern standards.

He probably engaged in activities like foraging, providing for and defending his family from predators, seeking or building shelter, relying on the strength of community, and making decisions about migration to improve his living conditions and secure an uncertain future. He would have planned and designed his life and future within the limits of his abilities and those of his community.

In many ways, his goals and objectives wouldn't have been much different from what we aim to achieve in our own lives. These similarities lead us to conclude that the foundations of the modern world, as we know it today, trace back to the caves and fields of the Upper Paleolithic period.

The perception that the primitive man exhibited sophistication from the very beginning is supported by several anthropologists and scholars. Early humans had complex social structures and cultural practices. The figurative paintings on the walls of the caves that they inhabited claim an artistic sense similar to that of modern humans. Despite lacking the most basic tools, paintings, pottery, decorative accessories, burial remains, weapons, and countless artefacts found at archeological sites suggest that early humans were not just simple or unsophisticated. These records argue that *Homo sapiens* had intricate social systems, rituals, and ways of understanding the world around them. We often see early humans as a separate group, distant from our modern reality and living simpler lives. Yet, their tracks clearly show they were our ancestors.

Occupational skills from the past are responsible for the building up of our modern civilization. Hunter-gatherers would eventually give way to farmers and the development of communities which required the skill of builders, blacksmiths, carpenters, pottery-makers, herbalists, bakers, and stone masons. Community life demanded order which was implemented by the scribes through the keeping of records and by orators, advocators, and judges who acted as pacifiers during disputes. The association of artisans or merchants brought about confraternities or guilds which developed and evolved into what we know today as the professions.

Even though we still have guilds—or associations—the tradition of parents passing on the skills of an art and the knowledge of a trade to their children has largely been replaced by training provided in educational or vocational institutions. To top it all, new discoveries and advances in every known field have not only driven familial apprenticeship away but also demand constant specialization and certification, emphasizing the need for personal resilience and continuous learning.

Blueprints of Human Achievements

Current circumstances make modern life much more exciting compared to the challenging demands faced by the Jebel man.

Today, extreme specialization is required. Professional associations demand certifications that were unheard of just a few years ago—it's not only occupations, but even a simple food stall at an annual fair now requires public health certification. Interacting with people from different languages, races, countries, cultural backgrounds, and training makes communication skills a real challenge. The overwhelming flood of data, information, and opinions from media across various platforms makes assimilation nearly impossible.

We have discovered and, to some extent, believe that basic management principles—such as leadership, communication, capacity building, problem-solving, financial management, and planning—can help us become better and more fulfilled individuals. There is some truth to this.

Throughout human history, the greatest engineering achievements—bridges, buildings, aviation, automobiles, and more—have required meticulous analysis, research, and innovation. The greatest exploration feats of the past and the present required not just a strategy and courage but prudence too because the lives of the explorers were and are usually at stake. And so, the showdown between Roald Amundsen[14] and Robert Falcon Scott for the honor of being the first to reach the South Pole highlighted the critical importance of leadership and managerial skills. Amundsen reached the pole on December 14, 1911, while Scott arrived later, on January 17, 1912.

This is a classy story often used to show how crucial research, planning, and innovation play a part. Scott thought that a Wolseley motorized sled and

26—Management

Manchurian ponies would bring him to the South Pole faster and safely—which proved to be wrong because he had to abandon them before the climb of the Beardmore Glacier. Amundsen used them too but only to approach it; he would eventually leave them along the way to run sled dogs and reach the Pole.

Fig. 11: South Pole, December 14, 1911 (Olav Bjaaland. From *De Aarde en haar Volken*, 1913. Public Domain via Wikimedia Commons).

Amundsen developed a vitamin-based diet against scurvy, which Scott contracted during the expedition, slowing down his progress. Amundsen thought of leaving provisions within strategic short distances from each other. Scott, on the other hand, left the supply depots farther apart, and, unable to reach them during a storm, this ultimately cost him his life. The odds turned against Scott too who, presumably, hit by a severe blizzard[15] died in his tent.

Many believe that the tragic death of Scott and his team on their return journey inspired Amundsen to attempt a rescue of his former expedition partner, Umberto Nobile, years later. Driven by a sense of duty and camaraderie among explorers, Amundsen tragically lost his life during the attempt, and his body was never recovered.

Amundsen learned to use—and managed to apply—modern managerial skills that enabled him to successfully reach the South Pole; there is no point of contention here. You might add luck to the equation, but as Seneca reminds us, "Luck is what happens when preparation meets opportunity."

A Case for Managing Your Life

There are parallels between exploration and the journey of life. A well-defined, clear plan of action is needed to make sense and drive us to a thrilling type of existence. Perhaps we have never thought about this, but to make things happen, we need a plan. Age influences how we plan. Younger people need to turn their imagination into achievable steps, while older individuals must always face uncertainties. No matter the age, thoughtful planning is key to turning dreams into reality, with each stage requiring a different approach.

As of 2024, the average global life expectancy is approximately 73.3 years—70.7 years for males, and 76.0 years for females—which is a significant improvement over historical periods when you were not expected to live beyond 40. This can vary significantly depending on the country and region. Localities like Hong Kong and Japan top the list with a life expectancy over 84 years, while in some other regions, it can be as low as 54.[16] Still, "there is no evidence that the span of human life has increased since the beginning of recorded history. Neither is there any evidence that the death rate of centenarians has decreased."[17]

The need to make the most of our time brings up an important question: Are the goals we set for ourselves truly worth pursuing? A good friend of mine recently retired from the only company he had ever worked for. It was his first job, and after forty years, he had climbed the corporate ladder, making significant contributions in accounting and purchasing, and transforming his department into a highly efficient unit. After his retirement party he went home and did not know what to do. The person who replaced him and his former team recognized his contributions but soon moved in their own direction, changing the systems he had developed. Were his forty years of work truly valuable? Is productivity the only goal of work?

While statistical data on productivity is ambiguous, Patrick Aubert's analysis provides some clarity. "We find that productivity increases with age until age 40 and then remains stable after this age. Workers aged 40 and more are roughly 5% more productive than workers aged 35-39, while workers below 30 are 15% to 20% less productive."[18] On the other hand, intellectual and creative output peaks between the ages of 60 and 70. This period is often associated with a wealth of experience, knowledge, and expertise that can significantly enhance intellectual performance. The second most productive stage is from 70 to 80 years of age.[19]

Interesting. Considering employment and evolving responsibilities within the organization we work for, these two periods of our life—the physical and the intellectual—can stage the focus and the type of activity we might likely enjoy more. This understanding could have given a twist to the problem of my friend and added more meaning to his life after retirement. It can happen to us too.

We devote our whole life to work. We spend years and years in tasks that bring only a temporary satisfaction. Perhaps, we won't realize that our life was sort of meaningless until later, when we retire and have more time to reflect on it.

Commonly understood, management is a process that leads us to becoming successful in life. However, what is success? What does it mean to be truly successful? Success can be defined as the achievement of that which holds value and meaning for an individual. It is deeply personal and varies widely depending on one's aspirations, values, and perspectives.

We do believe that success leads to happiness and so we search for it tirelessly. For some, happiness might mean attaining wealth, career milestones, or recognition. For others, it may be about nurturing relationships, or making a positive impact on the world. It could also be as simple yet profound as living authentically and enjoying peace of mind.

The legend of the magpie parallels that of the crow. Both bird species are said to collect shiny objects or non-food items.

Fig. 12: The legend of the magpie.

As intelligent as they are, their actions seem driven by curiosity rather than greed. According to the unconfirmed legend, they carry their finds to their nests, keeping them as trophies to admire and protect. Similarly, when our planning makes us hoard rather than share, we start acting like magpies—collecting everything in sight and never knowing when to stop.

To avoid becoming magpie holders, we need to infuse significance into our designs. We need to understand what drive us to be successful.

Success and happiness remain an elusive goal that everyone chases. Every action we take, every choice we make, is often driven by our relentless pursuit of this universal quest for success. What does success look like for you?

The Importance of Planning

Managerial skills will undoubtedly transform us into achievers, but they may lead to contentment rather than true happiness. Happiness is found in the balance of making sense, in the process of discovering meaning and significance—which is the central theme explored throughout the pages of this book. However, among the most basic and essential skills needed to get started and make progress, planning takes the lead.

Stephen R. Covey tells us that success is driven by habits. In his book *The 7 Habits of Highly Effective People*, Covey emphasizes the role of planning and goal setting as essential habits for achieving success. His framework for personal and professional growth emphasizes the need of staging progress into manageable steps and setting clear and precise objectives to avoid chasing unattainable dreams.

Years ago, during my mandatory military service—or draft, I was stationed at a training camp outside my hometown, within a giant military reserve—at least, it looked to me that way. Our instruction covered every aspect of the military life, survival, and war games.

Our Captain, a transfer from an especial forces division, wanted to make our training truly unique.

32—Management

And so, we crawled under live machinegun fire, escaped from enclosed areas hit by smoke grenades, fired all types of weapons imaginable, disassembled and assembled our rife in the dark, and learned many other skills which, I assume, did not belong to the standard military training offered in the camp.

Fig. 13: The idea was to execute a tactical maneuver over a hilly terrain.

One night, we were ordered to camouflage. We applied face paint, covered weapons to prevent any shine or reflection, secured loose gear that might make noise, and broke up our silhouette, especially around the head and shoulders, to avoid standing out against the landscape. Failure to comply meant weekend arrest and services in the camp. It was a war game.

The company was divided into squads and given mission orders—'any other soldier outside your squad is to be treated as enemy and avoided.' The idea was to execute a tactical maneuver over a hilly terrain of around ten kilometers. We were given four cardinal directions and distances to cover, marking three waypoints using a compass and map. We started at 12 midnight, and we had to be back at 4 a.m. Our unit arrived at 6 a.m. ... We were the first ones. The Captain, clearly exasperated, exclaimed, 'Great. Just great. What have you learned in the last three months of your training!'— he actually used much stronger language which, I feel, is inappropriate to write.

We *marshal* progress by setting goals and objectives, much like cardinal coordinates, which are essential for navigation and orientation. Just as cardinal coordinates are used with a map or compass to determine direction and location, we combine goals, objectives, and strategies to achieve success. What are the cardinal coordinates of your plan? Your coordinates must align to reach the intended destination.

Now that we've mapped the coordinates, we need to look at the navigator. What must we refine in ourselves to move confidently toward our goals? This shift—from planning to personal growth—opens the door to the next chapter: Essentials.

Chapter Three: Essentials

A desire for improvement clearly indicates the value one places on personal development—a trait that typically manifests as maturity, responsibility, and a strong sense of character.

But what of the individuals who dodge responsibility in favor of an easier, complication-free existence? This refusal to 'grow up'—to trade comfort for maturity—is famously known as the *Peter Pan Syndrome*.

Fig. 14: The Peter Pan Syndrome.

The Scottish playwright and novelist J.M. Barrie is best known for creating Peter Pan, the boy who lived in the mythical Never-Never Land, where children never grow up. While those with *Peter Pan Syndrome* can and do reach adulthood, they remain stubbornly resistant to embracing the responsibilities that come with it.

The *Peter Pan Syndrome*, also known as 'failure to launch,' is characterized by avoiding responsibilities and commitment, struggling to develop deeper and mature relationships, exhibiting childish behavior and attitudes, and always on the lookout for fun and thrills, dodging essential matters. Don't be a Peter Pan.

Fig. 15: Roald Amundsen
(Anonymous, Public Domain via Wikimedia Commons).

Greatness is built on our personal effort to develop ourselves to achieve the goals and objectives we have set in life.

In his autobiography *My Life as an Explorer*, Amundsen writes that from age 15 onward he began preparing for a life of polar exploration, spending every free moment outdoors in winter to toughen himself.[20]

Another biographical source notes that as a boy he kept his bedroom windows open at night, no matter what the weather, specifically to accustom himself to the cold.[21]

Every protagonist in the annals of historical achievements carries within a story of self-denial and labor.

The historical free solo climb of *El Capitan* was not a surprise for anyone who knew the intense training of Alex Honnold. He tackled the 3,000-foot climb (or 914 m, 5.13a route) on June 3, 2017, and successfully reached the summit in just 3 hours and 56 minutes.

He had done the same route dozens of times before with ropes and partners to memorize every single move. He prepared mentally and physically. Because the wall is sheer granite, he worked on finger strength in particular and maintained a high level of cardiovascular fitness.[22]

We know of others—many of them anonymous to the rest of the world—who, despite poverty, sickness, physical limitations, and odd circumstances, have turned their constraints into strengths and achieved their dreams.

This is true, not only for those who managed to leave a mark in sports, science, literature, and every other field, but also for fathers and mothers, professionals, entrepreneurs, skill workers, masters, specialists, and experts who have worked to become what they now proudly are

Fig. 16: AI-generated illustration of the free solo climb of *El Capitan*.

Personal Development Literature

Many have achieved their dreams through sheer effort and wits. Many more today count on the help of numerous modern writers who have mastered the skill and transcribed their findings into writing for us all to enjoy.

The contribution of these authors is often categorized as Personal Development. Personal development literature focuses on practical designs aiding emotional regulation, productivity, interpersonal effectiveness, and self-leadership.

Best sellers speak about emotional management (Marie Kondo), balancing priorities (Stephen Covey), time management (David Allen), interpersonal skills (Dale Carnegie), personal mastery (Robin Sharma), and other specialized tools and skills developed by experts.

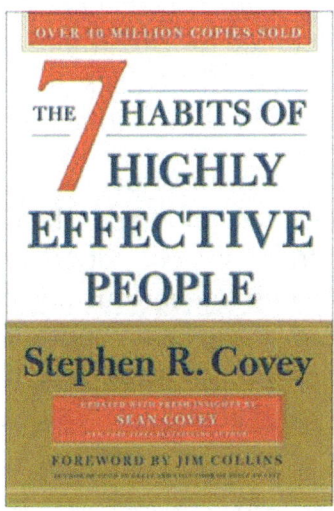

Fig. 17: The standout best-seller of the personal development genre, with over 40 million copies sold.

Marie Kondo on Emotional Management

Works: *The Life-Changing Magic of Tidying Up: The Japanese Art of Decluttering and Organizing* (published for first time in 2010, more than 11 million copies sold).

In her book, she teaches that your emotional world deserves the same care as your physical space, and that unprocessed feelings can clutter the mind just like objects clutter a room. Her healing process starts by asking whether something "sparks joy." Her therapy recommends "letting go"—whether of objects or old emotions.

Stephen Covey's Balancing Priorities

Works: *The 7 Habits of Highly Effective People* (published for first time in 1989, more than 40 million copies sold) and *First Things, First* (published for first time in 1994, more than 2 million copies sold).

Covey teaches that most people confuse urgency with importance, which traps them in constant reactivity and stress. By consciously reducing time spent on distractions (urgent but not important) and time-wasters (neither urgent nor important), you regain control of your schedule and align your days with your long-term values and goals.

David Allen on Time Management

Works: *Getting Things Done: The Art of Stress-Free Productivity* (published for first time in 2001, more than 2 million copies sold).

Your mind is for having ideas, not holding them — so you must capture everything that has your attention in a trusted system. His GTD (Getting Things Done) method follows five steps: Capture, Clarify, Organize, Reflect, and Engage — a workflow that turns chaos into clarity and action.

Dale Carnegie on Interpersonal Skills

Works: *How to Win Friends and Influence People* (published for first time in 1936, more than 30 million copies sold).

He teaches that effective relationships begin with genuine interest in others, not self-promotion. His core message is, treat people with warmth, curiosity, and respect, and influence naturally follows.

Robin Sharma on Personal Mastery

Works: *The Monk Who Sold His Ferrari* (published for first time in 1996, more than 6 million copies sold) and *Personal Mastery* (published for first time in 2015, millions sold across the series).

Personal mastery begins with self-awareness, the courage to look inward, and the discipline to grow daily. He emphasizes habit transformation. He teaches that leadership starts with leading yourself first. The ultimate goal is to unlock your potential and live with purpose, service, and impact.

The Shape of Modern Literature

The landscape of authors is much broader than the big names most people recognize. What's striking is how many thinkers, across different eras and disciplines, have shaped what we now call personal development, personal effectiveness, or self-leadership literature. When you zoom out, you see a heritage rather than a list.

We can summarize their lessons in a simple line: the goal of each of these techniques is self-satisfaction and happiness. Every writer ultimately concludes that happiness is found in the balance of making sense—in the ongoing process of discovering meaning and significance.

The latest addition to personal development is the understanding of how character is developed and mastered. Nothing being written today on the subject is truly original. Aristotle started it all. He proclaimed a gradual transformation of character built through habitual good actions. Aristotle nailed it: his ideas laid the foundation for modern personal development.

Modern pioneers such as Carl Rogers (1902–1987), Abraham Maslow (1908–1970), Jean Piaget (1896–1980), and Erik Erikson (1902–1994) successfully expanded Aristotle's idea into influential theories on the stages of human development. Later in the 20th century, educators like Michael Josephson and Curtis Florence identified and proposed models for character development.

The Five Pillars of Character

However, only recently has Carlos Beltrano integrated and summarized the work of his predecessors in his innovative conceptualization of the five pillars of character. "Character is not, therefore, a univocal concept but a broad, multifaceted one. It can be said that character can be understood from different complementary points of view... Putting these aspects together in a complementary way, it can be said that they are like five pillars that support and define character education as a whole." [23]

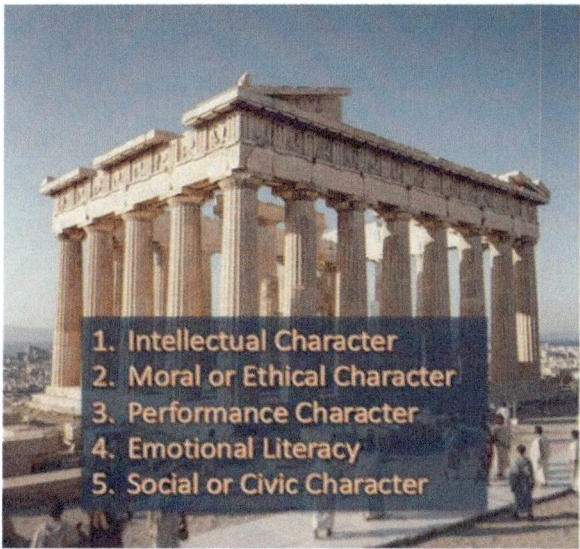

Fig. 18: The Five Pillars of Character
(Conceptualized by Carlos Beltramo)

Intellectual Character guides and develops reflective thinking—a capacity every human being can cultivate when given proper training.

Moral and ethical character encourages thoughtful and responsible behavior by fostering the ability to understand the consequences of each of our actions.

Performance Character nurses a steady disposition to draw strength, ability, and motivation from any favorable or adverse circumstance.

Emotional Literacy bridges the gap between subjective emotional responses and objective human realities, helping us understand both more clearly.

Social or Civic Character integrates our personal cognitive and emotional capacities so we can engage meaningfully and responsibly with others.

Further explanations on the five pillars of character are presented and developed extensively in the book *Why Character?*, which each of you is encouraged to read as a complement to this work on Life Management.[24]

Why Life Management Matters

Personal development is intimately related to life management. Life management is driven not only by knowledge—something that we will explore in the following chapters—but a personal attitude and the values needed to be successful in every labor.

Considering the importance given today to personal development theories, their treatment and practical applications, we could say that we are witnessing the emergence of a new science, which we have started calling *Life Management*.

All these considerations outline the reasons for writing a book on *Life Management*.

Life Management is more than just handling personal projects: it's a holistic approach to managing every aspect of life, such as personal, professional, financial, health, family and relationships. It's a strategy for balancing and improving all areas to achieve overall well-being and fulfillment.

It involves making thoughtful choices and taking intentional actions to reach sustainable aspirations and dreams. It benefits from essential skills like time management, goal setting, stress management, and self-discipline.

Management is widely understood as *the coordination and administration of tasks to achieve a goal.* [25] Yet, management is different from life management, which contains it. Life is broader than management and the source of it.

Life management can be defined as the systematic analysis and organization of every aspect of our life that gives us the ability to balance what is meaningful and achieve unity of purpose, peace, and happiness.

"If we do not organize our lives, we run the risk of feeling lost, without direction, disoriented, without knowing what to expect. And this is terrible. What does it mean to feel lost? First of all, it alludes to the fact that one cannot find oneself, that one has not found the key to one's life and, therefore, is without a north, without a guiding point of reference."[26]

Areas of Interest

Managing our goals starts with sorting them into clear *Areas of Interest* and revisiting those categories as our priorities shift. It's a process of asking what truly matters and what each objective adds to the larger picture we're trying to shape. Yet the landscape isn't always honest. Some pursuits shine brightly at first glance but turn out to be distractions, pulling us away from the work that actually moves us forward.

Significance and relevance emerge within what we might call Context—the state, condition, or position we find ourselves in. Every other Area of Interest functions as a pillar of that Context, expressed through the meaningful goals we choose to pursue. These pillars reflect some of the most commonsense needs of modern life: Assessment, Security, and Capacity.

On account of this, we can outline our four areas of interest as

(1) *Context* — the projected sense and direction of our life.

(2) *Assessment* — comprising our assets, liabilities, and opportunities.

(3) *Security* — expressed through planning for an unpredictable future.

(4) *Capacity* — the skills and training that support the achievement of our broader targets.

To align our efforts with our most meaningful goals, we need to examine each area closely, break it into specific objectives, and use those steps to build steady progress.

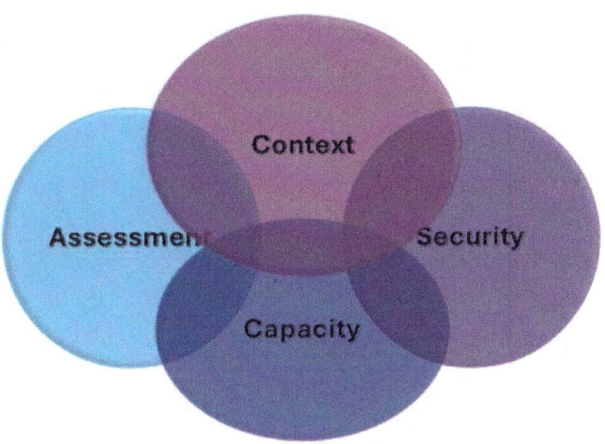

Fig. 19: Areas of Interest

Chapter Four: Context

When we talk about *Context*, we're referring to the situation we're in and the direction our life appears to be heading. It's shaped by our relationships, our sense of meaning, and the values we choose to uphold. Among all the *Areas of Interest*, this one sits at the top. It frames everything else.

Context is often forgotten when success becomes the only purpose of one's life. The focus on performance and money—and the power it gives—is shifting attention away from important values like love, friendship, and family, turning people more selfish and self-centered.

We know of people who, having reached the pinnacle of success in their lives, are unable to enjoy it because of their messy lifestyles and the hollow values that they pursue. Often, we see how the rich, the glamorous, celebrities, artists, and even popular athletes struggle with finding purpose or meaning in their achievements. However, their success is eclipsed by feelings of isolation and disconnection from their loved ones.

True success and fulfillment in life are tied up to circumstances around our commitments and the values we live for—which are interdependent from each other. Let me just add that our Context is characterized by the true value of our goals. This might seem unusual or puzzling to some, but think about it.

We are familiar with the life of sportsmen and women, movie stars, politicians, businessmen and women, and other public figures who ruined their life pursuing the wrong values. The list of those is endless.

Some of you might remember Lance Armstrong, who after surviving cancer and winning seven Tour de France titles, was stripped of those victories and banned for life following extensive doping investigations—legal battles soon followed..

Fig. 20: AI-generated illustration of the infamous 1997 bout.

Mike Tyson's career might have reached even greater heights were it not for his 1992 rape conviction and several well-known incidents of violence, including the infamous moment when he bit part of Evander Holyfield's ear during their 1997 fight.

Despite her glamorous exterior, Marilyn Monroe's life, raising to fame as a Hollywood icon and sex symbol, was marked by personal struggles and a tragic end.

On the milder side, we find the résumé embellishment of former Yahoo CEO Scott Thompson, who falsely claimed a computer science degree—a controversy that undermined trust in his leadership and contributed to turmoil within the company.

Was trading a life of dedication for a selfish dream ever worth it? Life's true richness does not lie in the mere physical satisfaction of achieving something at any cost, regardless of who bears the consequences. Richness is attained by respecting ethical and universal laws coexisting side by side with a physical, natural world with laws of its own.

To this end we need realistic goals without defective values. This is perhaps where many have failed, misjudging their uncontrollable passions, confusing anti-values for values, at a breakneck speed and without safety nets.

Without recognizing the ultimate ethical values we live for, we risk pursuing an endless series of goals, achieving every objective along the way but ultimately getting nowhere, like chasing illusions or dreaming over dreams.

Think of the years we have let pass by: what values did we truly live for? Think of the years ahead: can we discern the direction we are moving toward and the steps we need to take? Do our objectives align with ethical standards? Can we, with sincerity, identify what truly motivates us?

Relationship and Family

Relationships and family are among the simplest examples highlighting the significance and purpose of life.

Most humans inhabiting this world find in the family the ultimate value of their life. The deepest longing of a man or a woman is to love and be loved, and this is usually accomplished within family boundaries. If this is your condition, your goals and objectives would prioritize not just finances but family values as well.

It is crucial to understand that the "Family is the bedrock of our lives. It is the place we return to for love, understanding, commitment, and a sense of belonging."[27] Many had forgotten or ignored this out loud principle, ending up with an apparent success devoid of meaning. In family life, the rewards of love and dedication are always significant; when obstacles arise, the challenges are always worth facing and overcoming.

However, not everyone is motivated by kinship. Some have other plans involving big projects, research, and enterprises demanding years of dedication and hard work.

For many single people, the search takes them down all kinds of paths — from figuring out what they really want to unexpectedly meet someone who might matter.

Others dedicate their lives to caring for a sick or disabled relative, engaging in a spiritual pursuit, managing a family business, or working on a project aimed at improving the welfare of others.

Fig. 21: The rewards of love and dedication are always significant.

Whatever our circumstances, we need to plan around what truly matters. And when our goals start pulling us away from the values we want to live by, we have to find the courage to change courses.

Relevance

Relevance gives meaning to whatever goal we have set for ourselves. Still, as pointed out earlier, the ultimate relevant value is love and love demands reciprocity.

If your passion is, for example, astronomy and you devote yourself to search and research as the ultimate purpose of your life, excluding everything else, you should understand that the stars don't love back, your publications don't love back, your professional contacts don't love back ... Your ego does not reciprocate love simply because it cannot. You are just one reality, not two (unless you are suffering from schizophrenia).

Fig. 22: 'Who cares!'

My ego, your ego. Maybe neither of us cares. But what exactly are we refusing to care about? 'I don't care' can come from selfishness, sure, yet it can just as easily be a declaration of resolve when our efforts go unnoticed.

The latter interpretation is the correct one. We don't concern ourselves with what others think because our goals are right, and we are determined to pursue them.

In this sense, if the value of our study or work leads to advancements in science that ultimately benefit many, we may have found a truly worthy purpose in life. If our efforts result in an act of service to a group of people, we may have discovered the reciprocity of love we've been searching for.

We have considered context within permanent values such as family, work, and service, based on personal attitudes toward lifelong goals. But what about temporary relationships? What can we say about temporary associations, such as membership in an institution, business partnerships, or a transient live-in situation? How could you plan for the future of two or more people who will eventually separate ways?

Definitely, you will only plan for yourself. A temporary association within an institution, cohabitation, or a business partnership is never a priority in a life management plan. While there are certainly reasons behind any fleeting relationship, business connection, or temporary membership, life management focuses on the permanent, as it is deeply personal and centered on individual goals and objectives.

Because of the especially intimate and emotional but transient conditions of a live-in situation, we need to deal with it separately.

A relationship of this type equates to excluding a life partner from one's deepest personal alliances, making that person useful but disposable, outside one's own personal life and interest. This is real but difficult to accept and humiliating for the person who feels betrayed in a sincere relationship. People who follow this path often end up living independent but lonely lives, regretting years of isolation without companionship.

Let's move forward with our strategy and outline a method for clearing the mind and understanding the motivations, challenges, and values that shape our decisions.

Value-Driven Life Management

Make two lists. The first list contains the challenges you are currently facing. The second list—mirroring these challenges—highlights the values that each challenge represents. Next, use these challenges and values to reflect, analyze, prioritize, and formulate an action plan aligned with the general recommendations provided in this book. You may need to realign and even establish a new set of objectives, breaking them down into manageable steps.

You can see how the process works in the practical example that follows.

1. LIST OF CHALLENGES. Note down the challenges that you're currently facing.

- Keeping up with work demands
- Finding time to specialize further or improve certain skills
- Increasing savings to secure my family's future
- Deepening my relationship with my spouse
- Making more time for rest and relaxation
- Building stronger connections with my colleagues

2. IDENTIFY THE VALUES represented by each challenge:

- Work demands → Resilience
- Improving skills → Time management
- Increasing family savings → Planning
- Relationship with your spouse → Quality time
- Rest and relaxation → Balance
- Connecting with colleagues → Time off

3. ANALYZE your challenges:

➢ The main issue is time management.
➢ Priority should be given to the most important value in my life: my spouse.
➢ Resilience is key to achieving my objectives.

4. PRIORITIZE. Arrange challenges according to the analysis of values:

- Relationship with your spouse → Quality time

- Work demands → Resilience
- Increasing family savings → Planning
- Improving skills → Time management
- Rest and relaxation → Balance
- Connecting with colleagues → Time off"

5. ACTION PLAN. Outline the steps needed to achieve each goal. If possible, break them down into smaller, manageable tasks:

- Relationship with my spouse → Have a weekly date night and call him or her during the day; make it a priority to be home by 9:00 PM, no matter what.
- Work demands → Wake up one hour earlier each day, which means no TV during weekdays to ensure I go to bed earlier. Stay positive at the office and avoid complaints.
- Increasing family savings → Set aside time once a month to review and plan for savings and possible investments. Bring up the topic with friends or consider seeking professional advice.
- Improving skills → Dedicate a little time every day to learning more about spreadsheets while working on tasks in the office.
- Rest and relaxation → Plan a family outing once a month. We'll discuss this during our evening family gatherings.
- Connecting with colleagues → Spend my lunch break with colleagues instead of eating alone.

Check in on your progress regularly and adjust along the way. Life shifts, and your plan should be able to shift with it.

Fig.23: Value-driven Life Management

The Importance of Keeping a Diary

A great aid to a life management project is the keeping of a diary. The habit of writing down thoughts and facts about significant moments in your life releases stress and anxiety, makes us more analytical and productive, boosts motivation and reflection. You can note down snippets from this reading to turn them into goals and objectives, your plans, and keep them at hand.

There are many good reasons for keeping a diary. For first timers, "Regular writing is known to reduce symptoms of depression and anxiety, and it can be used as a form of stress and emotional regulation."[28]

You don't need to be so demanding as to impose a daily writing schedule—which in the end will add anxiety and stress you even further. You only need to write things down when, in your opinion, facts and personal feelings are important and should be noted down.

Fig. 24: There are many good reasons for keeping a diary.

Keeping a diary is one way of benefiting mental wellbeing. The need to blow off steam, unwind, unburden oneself, cool off, unload, and relax demands it. It also forces you to place your analytical mind to work and find reasons behind your feelings or the facts that you credit. If you find it bothersome, don't pay too much attention to style and grammar—which autocorrect options in electronic devices can actually facilitate it. Focus on how clear facts and thoughts are expressed. Concentrate on the honest part of yourself.

"Writing in a diary can help you prioritize tasks and make a plan for the day, which can lead to increased productivity. Productive people tend to have a system of organization that works for them. Writing can help you structure your week such that you carve out time for all the entries on your to-do list."[29] A diary helps analyze and organize your thoughts. It could be of great aid for a life management project.

Fig. 25: Electronic devices make it easy to take and update notes.

Today, technology offers the simplest and easiest way of keeping any record private by the use of access codes or passwords. You can easily find more than a hundred diary applications across all commercial platforms, designed to meet your needs and match the level of sophistication you aspire to.

Develop the habit of noting down the most relevant events about your life together with your plans and your insights. Every passage in your diary should be headed by the date—and perhaps even the place where you find yourself at the moment.

Chapter Five: Assessment

This area of interest explores the assets at your disposal, along with your liabilities and opportunities. Are you employed? Are you financially stable? Are you in debt? What resources can you rely on? Dreams, employment, personal goals, a professional career, and plans for a future abroad must all come together as part of your life management strategy.

We all dream of better and more lucrative employment which is often both possible and unrealistic. No one can claim clairvoyance, but we often talk about fate. Fate is shaped by our abilities and opportunities, which include job and investment prospects. We'll discuss this further in the next chapter.

Lucrative Employment

Lucrative employment opportunities can be found in sectors such as finance, technology, healthcare, consulting, and freelancing. When it comes to investment opportunities, many people seek profitable income sources in the following areas: the stock market and dividends (including cryptocurrency); crowdfunding; real estate and rental properties; peer-to-peer lending; small businesses; and the selling of digital products such as e-books, courses, software, together with other side ventures.[30]

64—Assessment

Perhaps the extended but still incomplete list of lucrative areas might sound like a foreign language to many but don't feel challenged. Explore what they mean and find out if a new interest and capacitation can expand the horizon of your work and employment.

Fig. 26: Generally high-paying fields.

Your line of work is your highway. However, remember that all highways have traffic signs limiting your speed, telling you to turn right or left when needed, warning you of slippery surfaces, and pointing in the direction you must follow to get to your destination.[31]

All of us have commitments. Commitments, and the way you respond to the obligations that your state imposes on you, limit the freedom that you might be expecting in a highway. But don't see this limitation as something negative. When you ignore warning signals in a highway you are chancing accidents and even courting death. You need to see your plans, employment, or career within the loving needs of those who depend on you.

Professional work, commitments, and obligations should be integrated into a personal finance plan, as neglecting them can lead to disastrous consequences.

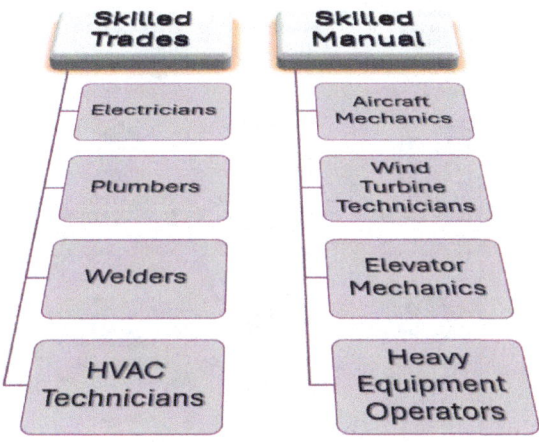

Fig. 27: Potential Lucrative Occupations.

Although difficult to track precisely, homelessness continues to rise each year in most countries. Aside from natural disasters, the primary causes include unemployment, a lack of affordable housing, and rising eviction rates.

While it's important not to take a pessimistic or alarmist view of personal finances, this reality underscores the need for strategic planning. Experts recommend several basic strategies to help manage debts, such as mortgages, loans, and credit cards, effectively.[32]

Fig. 28: Personal finances also benefit from the core principles of strategic planning.

The figure above can help you grasp the complexity of this process and highlight key stages you may be overlooking. We're not going to cover the entire strategic planning process — instead, we'll simplify it so you can start focusing on some aspects of personal financial planning.

Personal Financial Planning

First and foremost, financial advisers recommend personal financial planning to help you track your income and expenses, including debt management when applicable. This is both practical and essential. By tracking your income and expenses, you gain a clear picture of your financial situation, allowing you to adjust as needed.

Income, Expenses, and Savings

Personal finance is something we all need to keep an eye on. While basic financial principles can be straightforward, they may still require some effort to learn and apply effectively.

Personal Finance TRACKER		Jan		Feb	
		CASH	CREDIT	CASH	CREDIT
INCOME	**YTD**				
Salary	$48,000.00	$4,000.00		$4,000.00	
Bonus	$5,500.00				
Sales	$12,000.00	$1,000.00		$1,000.00	
Dividends	$0.00				
Other Income	$12,400.00	$500.00		$300.00	
TOTAL INCOME	**$77,900.00**	$5,500.00		$5,300.00	
EXPENSES	**YTD**				
Insurance	$1,800.00	$150.00		$150.00	
Water, Electricity	$2,292.50	$196.70		$150.20	
Cable	$240.00	$20.00		$20.00	
Mobile Network Operators	$240.00	$20.00		$20.00	
Exercise	$0.00				
Garden	$0.00				
Medical	$384.00	$28.00			
Academics	$0.00				
Rent	$12,000.00	$1,000.00		$1,000.00	
Food and Groceries	$8,690.00	$350.00	$350.00	$250.00	$600.00
Food & Beverage Outings	$3,680.00	$400.00		$200.00	
Entertainment	$1,970.00	$100.00	$0.00	$50.00	$100.00
Childcare	$4,800.00	$150.00	$250.00	$150.00	$250.00
Clothing	$1,720.00		$200.00	$200.00	
Other Expenses	$0.00				
PARTIAL EXPENSES	**$37,816.50**	$2,414.70	$800.00	$2,190.20	$950.00
TOTAL EXPENSES	**$63,567.21**	$5,414.70		$5,340.20	

Fig. 29: An example of a Personal Finance Tracker.

The more important categories to include in a spreadsheet are income, expenses, and savings.

Income

Income collects all the cash inflows you generate monthly. Depending on your age and situation, this category typically includes salaries, bonuses, pensions, as well as returns from passive investments, side jobs, or other sources of income.

Expenses

Expenses track every payment you make for essentials, services, insurance, and recreation. If you alternate between cash and credit for your purchases, be sure to distinguish between them, typically by using two separate columns. This is easily done with manual recording.

Savings

To secure your future, you'll need money. Savings represent the extra cash you set aside.

Debt Management

If you have debts, prioritize those with the highest interest rates—such as credit card payments, which can often be negotiated with the bank if you have a good credit history—to minimize total interest paid. Alternatively, paying off smaller debts first can build momentum and motivation. For multiple debts, consider consolidating them into a single loan with a lower interest rate, simplifying the number of payments to manage.

Bank loans typically have lower interest rates compared to credit cards. Personal loans from banks often come with fixed interest rates, which are generally lower because they are installment loans paid over a set period. Credit cards, on the other hand, usually have higher interest rates due to their revolving credit nature and the use of compound interest.

Secondly, seek motivation and advice. You may have relatives, friends, or acquaintances with the know-how who can guide you in budgeting or debt management. If you have many financial obligations, consider consulting a professional for tailored advice.[33]

What is important is to avoid debts and limit credit card usage. Veterans often recommend minimizing credit card use while focusing on debt repayment to avoid increasing overall debt levels. The Saturday Night Live sketch, 'Don't Buy Stuff,' is a humorous, rather silly, take on personal finance that highlights the absurdity of buying things on credit without a plan to pay later. Featuring Steve Martin, Bill Hader, and Kristen Wiig, the sketch promotes a fictitious book titled 'Don't Buy Stuff You Cannot Afford.' Through deadpan humor, the book emphasizes a straightforward message: don't spend money you don't have. At one point, Kristen reads, 'If you don't have any money, you should not buy anything.' She then adds, 'Sounds interesting,' to which Steve replies, 'Sounds confusing!'[34]

Xin Lu, who moved from Yangzhou, China, to the U.S., shares that 'if you ever examined my attitudes toward money, you would see that I am undeniably Chinese.' He describes the principles he grew up with—common among Chinese immigrants worldwide: (1) frugality as a virtue, (2) saving as much as possible, (3) paying for things with cash, and (4) always seeking a bargain. Observing these habits can help us adopt a more mindful approach to spending, addressing an area that often challenges our financial stability.[35]

Even if your profession requires budgeting and accounting expertise, personal financial planning remains a tough nut to crack for most people, because it involves confronting a reality that, being personal, can trigger strong emotional responses. The bases of this exercise are simple though. Subtract your expenses from your income to gauge your monthly savings. The question is: what are the key concepts that should be included in a monthly income and expense plan? Income concepts are very basic and include monthly salary, bonuses, and other forms of income proceeding from, for example, sidelines or investments. The list of expenses always seems to grow though: rent, food, dining out, entertainment, childcare, clothing, vacations, obligations, and other miscellaneous costs. Develop the habit of tracking your personal finances, even if it feels uncomfortable at first. This skill will prepare you for a more challenging—and potentially stressful—task: budgeting.

Debt Trackers

Mortgages, loans, and credit card debts are commonly utilized to boost purchasing power and strengthen financial resources. However, these commitments demand careful evaluation and thorough research before finalizing any agreement. Evaluation entails reviewing the terms, conditions, and timelines, while research involves assessing the reliability of the financial institution and considering the feedback and experiences of others who have made similar commitments.

Debt repayment plans are based on projections and percentages. As illustrated in the figure below, the relationship between interest rates, monthly payments, and your opening balance provides a comprehensive view of your debt status. With this understanding, you can make informed adjustments and design an effective debt management strategy, determining both your ideal monthly deposit amount and the duration for which you plan to continue making payments.

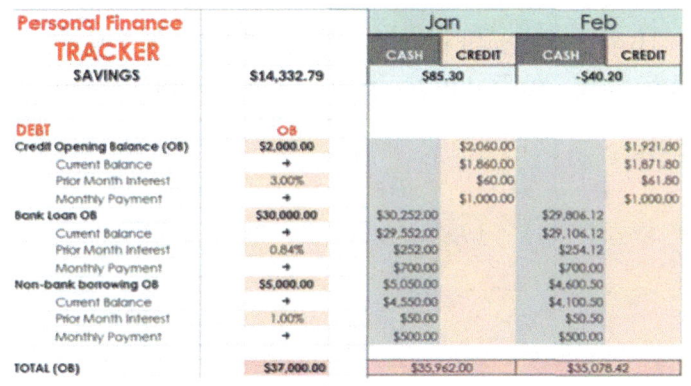

Fig. 30: An example of a Debt Tracker.

Debt track management should be integrated into your personal financial plans. This is particularly important if you are using credit cards instead of cash. Many people often fail to anticipate how the accumulation of debt encouraged by credit card usage can dramatically increase their monthly dues. If you are using credit cards, strive to minimize your dues whenever possible. Banks favor credit cards as a source of revenue, which includes promoting spending through special benefits regularly offered to clients. Credit cards also help banks ensure customer loyalty. Moreover, studies on spending habits provide insights that banks can leverage to sell to interested companies too.

The alternative to credit cards is debit cards. The banking system encourages the use of debit cards among clients who prefer more balanced, interest-free, and simpler account management. However, banks still earn revenue from transaction fees charged to merchants for debit card usage, similar to credit cards.

The key to debt management is to ensure that your debts don't push you to spend beyond your means.

Chapter Six: Security

The many groundbreaking achievements of Isaac Newton make him perhaps one of the most influential scientists of all time. His work in physics and mathematics, particularly his formulation of the laws of motion and universal gravitation, laid the foundation for significant advances in science. However, his statement 'What goes up must come down' has been a source of inspiration, not only in the understanding of gravity but also in the popular sense of destiny and futility (i.e., Blood, Sweat, and Tears' 1969 song, *Spinning Wheel*). Every one of us 'must come down' in a certain moment in time and everyone has to plan for that eventuality from the moment we become aware of the need—and even earlier—from the moment we become independent and start our own life.

Physical and mental health are always at risk. Financial needs vary, especially in times of crises. Long-term wealth-building strategies like saving, investing, or even debt management have to be tackled and brought down to managing incremental steps. It's well known that investing your savings is the most reliable way to secure an uncertain future.

Building a Great Financial Future

You can build a great financial future by planning, staying focused, and making wise choices. Numerous

74—Security

websites offer guidance on best practices. Below is a summary of expert recommendations, divided into three main areas that you may want to integrate into your plans.[36]

Fig. 31: Important areas to include in your plans.

Develop a budget

Here we have but a continuation of what we started developing under the heading Assessment. Track your earnings and expenses to understand your cash flow, and establish short-term (1–2 years), medium-term (3–5 years), and long-term (5+ years) goals to plan for major expenses like a home, retirement, or education for yourself or your family. Incorporate debt management into your budget, and aim to maintain current expense levels as your income grows. Take advantage of employer-sponsored plans when available, and prioritize retirement savings.

Save money for the unexpected.

Unexpected expenses can pop up at any time like repairs and medical bills. By setting aside a portion of your income regularly, you can build an emergency fund to avoid relying on loans. You could do so depositing a percentage of your monthly earnings in a separate account—ideally in an interest-earning investment. Aim to save enough to cover about five to six months of expenses for emergencies.

Get the right type of insurance.

There are various types, including health, life, disability, and property insurance. Although these can be high-cost investments, and not everyone may be able to afford full coverage, it's essential to understand the different types and their benefits. The right insurance can reduce tax burdens[37] or cover medical expenses that might otherwise deplete your emergency fund.

As a good family man or woman, you should also think about writing a will to designate beneficiaries and ensure that your assets go to the intended individuals—it is well-known that state laws can impede inheritance when beneficiaries are not explicitly named. In this line, you could also establish a power of attorney and healthcare directives to authorize someone to make decisions on your behalf if you become incapacitated.

It's a good idea to build strong financial habits. Pay your bills on time, keep your credit card balance low, and be mindful of your spending. But saving isn't enough. To truly secure your future, you need to plan for growth and make sure your finances work with your long-term goals and life situation.

Investment

The money you save is available for unexpected expenses or can be invested in profitable opportunities. This may be the most challenging aspect of financial planning, but don't get discouraged before giving in, try it out.

Investments are assets expected to generate income through commodities, bonds, stock market trading, real estate, or returns from venture capital. Other forms of investment include purchasing art or valuable items that appreciate in value over time.

In general, investing in the stock market is relatively uncommon. In Europe, aside from the United Kingdom, the percentage of the population participating in the stock market varies significantly by country. On average, 7.76% of Europeans invest in stocks, while 7.78% invest in investment funds. The highest participation rates are found in the United States, where 62% invest, followed by Canada at 49%, Australia at 37%, and the United Kingdom at 33%. In Asia, investment participation varies widely, ranging from 7% in most countries to 15% in Japan.

Regarding securities, the most popular form, insurance coverage, is growing significantly especially in emerging markets but again, it varies significantly by region and economic development. You can get insurance coverage for life or non-life insurance. Non-life insurance includes health, property, and casualty.

Popular Budgeting Methods

Given the wide range of readers interested in the topics explored in this book — with different needs and backgrounds — we can begin our discussion with simple yet practical budgeting systems.

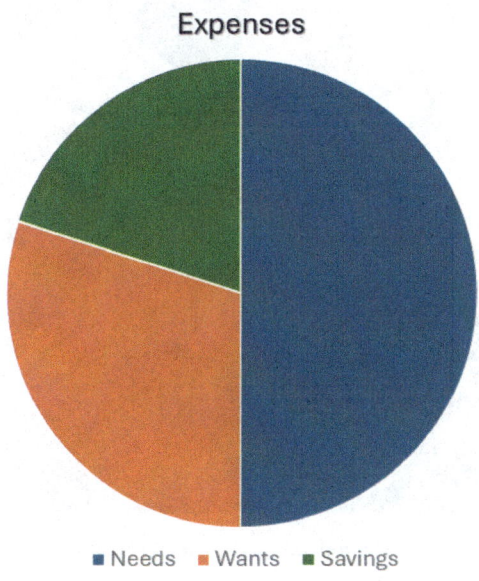

Fig. 32: The *50/30/20* Budget.

The 50/30/20 Budget

Few popular budgeting methods can be compared to the well-known *50/30/20 Budget*.

Based on percentage projection of expenses, it divides your income into three groups: *50% for needs,* covering essential expenses like rent, food, utilities, transportation, etc. *30% for wants*, also referred to as *discretional spending*, which includes dining out, entertainment, shopping, and hobbies. And *20% for savings and debt repayment*, like retirement funds, emergency funds, and loan repayments.

Fig. 33: Cash-based Envelop System.

The Envelop System

Monitor spending closely to ensure it aligns with the budget, but if you find this or any other known method too complicated, use the *envelop system* which is cash-based—or bank based if you use back accounts instead of envelopes.

This method allocates cash to different envelopes depending on the type of expense: you don't spend more than what is contained in the envelope. Of course, unplanned expenses could empty essentials like food or transportation, which recommends keeping your emergency fund envelope always at hand stashed with money.

Recording

The next step is to start writing things down — identifying our needs and organizing the information we're about to collect.

The simplest approach—developed in the previous chapter— records in a single spreadsheet the three most essential categories: income, expenses, and savings (which include both investments and other financial securities).

This basic structure is often referred to as a budget, especially when it includes future projections. In most cases, investment gains are counted as income, while costs related to financial protection — such as insurance — are recorded as expenses.

There are various tools available to help with the recording of income, expenses, and savings, ranging from simple to more complex. These tools can generally be classified into two categories: electronic solutions, such as apps and software, or traditional methods, which involve manual recording.

With the help of the software—and the chapter-five examples you've already explored—your personal finance plan will take shape just like the model shown in this section.

80—Security

There are several software options that offer free personal finance or budget templates. Microsoft 365[38] and Microsoft Create provide customizable personal budgeting templates that you can start using in Excel right after downloading them to your PC.

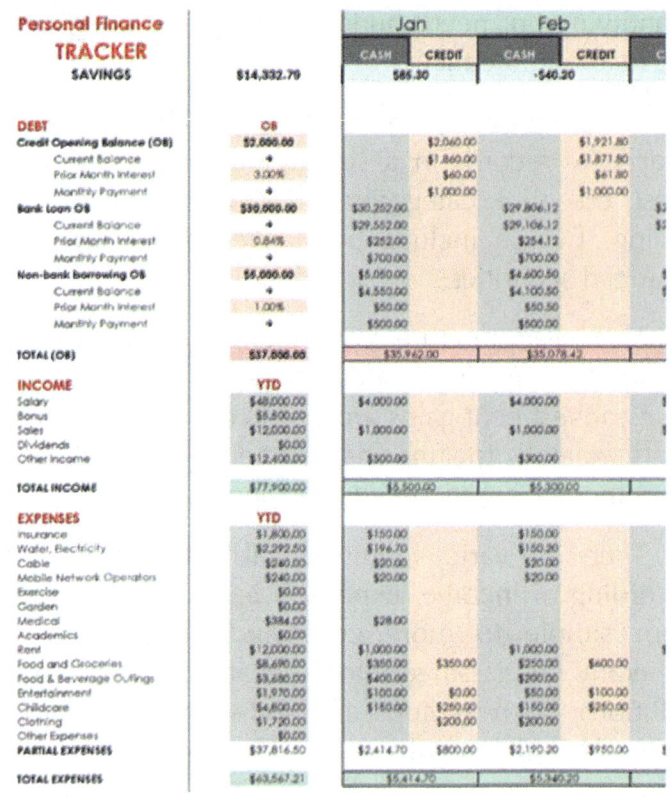

Fig. 34: Consolidating the Personal Finance Tracker.

Other free alternatives like AceMoney Lite (the free version of AceMoney), Mint (a free online budget planner), and Empower also offer financial tools you can use at your convenience. You can explore the options they offer and get familiar with their features.

Manual recording systems may seem simpler to some. You can find all kinds of forms at office supply stores and online marketplaces. If you regularly shop on e-commerce platforms, finding a ledger that suits your needs shouldn't be too difficult.

Fig. 35: Different types of ledgers.

Typically, ledgers feature a grid of rows and columns, which you can label for categories (rows) and months of the year (columns). You can also choose to record income and expenses as they occur, noting whether the payment was made in cash or credit.

Whether you prefer electronic or manual, pick the recording system that works best for you and start experimenting with it. You can also learn a bit more about financial terms using online resources. In the end, you'll see that personal finance and budgeting aren't as complicated as they seem, and you might even start enjoying it.

Chapter Seven: Capacity

No two newborn babies are alike; each one is a distinct individual with unique psychological and physical traits. Not even exact twins are equal. A newborn baby has roughly 2 trillion cells, while a typical adult has about 30 to 37 trillion cells. Our genetic makeup—the complete set of genes that define an organism—makes each of us unique in countless ways. In contrast to the precise duplication of even the most complex machines of our times, none of the 10 billion humans on Earth today can be replicated. Why? Big question. Scientists are trying, but the complexity and potential of a single embryo is something no technology can handle, and no scientist can truly grasp—let alone imitate. Care to wager on it?

In every ecosystem, the diversity of life, combined with the right environmental conditions, comes together to produce nature's marvelous wonders. Humans, in their natural ecosystem, can outdo nature. Every human has a place in our ecosystem. Each one of them, even those who may seem like a burden to the human ecosystem, has something to contribute—something that makes them unique.

The renowned Stephen William Hawking, an English theoretical physicist, cosmologist, and author, was a paraplegic. Ludwig van Beethoven one of the most famous composers was deaf. Helen Keller, though both deaf and blind, became a renowned author, political activist, and lecturer, inspiring many with her story of overcoming adversity. Mallory Weggemann, paralyzed from the waist down after an epidural injection, continued swimming and went on to break multiple world records and win multiple gold medals.

Fig. 36: Mallory Weggemann's 17th gold medal (Photo Courtesy, Nelson Books).

The list is endless. No one said it was easy. There is something remarkable in the human spirit that enables a person to overcome even the most apparent physical limitations and become a legend.

Everyone has some form of challenge to overcome. We must all work on addressing our weaknesses, disabilities, and uncovering our hidden talents. Personal development requires self-awareness, environmental insight, dedication to a purpose, methods to bridge knowledge gaps, and the refining touch of experience. Though not simple, it is achievable.

There is an aspect of personal growth—the unfolding of the richness of one's character—that we must examine. No matter how difficult or stressful, growth is essential for all of us. The connection between human growth and character development will be explored in another book entitled *Why Character?* but for now, we challenge ourselves by simply asking, 'What am I good at?'

What Are You Good At?

In both professional and social settings, the query 'What are your skills?' is a frequent topic of discussion. It is the standard measure of one's capabilities, potential, and worth. Today, the potential of fitting in a job is given by certification. However, within the professional path already shaped by fate—the opportunities that have come our way—we can always find something that aligns with our character, personality, and abilities. Perhaps what we first need is a deeper understanding of these capacities.

Personal capacities can be identified and summarized as follows:

Overall *physical condition*, fitness, stamina, and strength often determine the types of activities you can engage in, either limiting or expanding your options.

Adaptability and *flexibility*. The ability to cope with challenges and manage stress, adapt to change and uncertainty, and recover quickly from difficulties and setbacks.

Cognitive abilities like intelligence, problem-solving skills, creativity, and memory, together with Practical skills acquired out of necessity or as a hobby—such as management abilities, financial literacy, computer literacy, writing skills, and more.

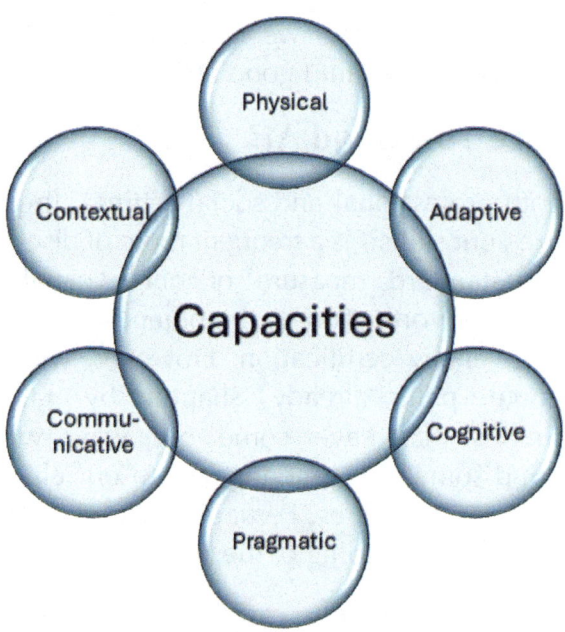

Fig. 37: Identifiable personal capacities.

Relational abilities, such as understanding and managing one's own emotions, empathizing with others, communication skills, and teamwork.

Confidence in one's own abilities to achieve goals and overcome obstacles and motivation to pursue them and persist in the face of challenges.

Lastly, let me add an uncommon layer to our discussion: the *in-context ability*, which refers to the capacity to respond to the responsibilities that any meaningful relationship imposes—whether as a fiancé, spouse, father, mother, or family member.

Reflect on all this and take a moment to question your current situation too. Whatever your job, background, or social condition, ask yourself: 'How did I get here? What does this journey reveal about me?' Consider the opportunities you've encountered and why some did not materialize. Then, note your conclusions and list the abilities you possess, along with the skills that can help you succeed.

Test Your Abilities

AI can help you analyze your abilities, suggest areas for growth, and identify types of work that may suit you well. To do this, we first group abilities by domain and mark each one with a checkmark indicating its level. These levels—high, standard (average), or low—reflect your own view of where you excel, where you feel less strong, and where you fall in the middle.

This exercise is confidential, so please avoid adding checkmarks to the table below. Instead, use the list provided in the appendix at the end of this chapter. You can make a copy of it and complete it separately. A clear photo of your filled-in sheet, along with the prompts that begin the exercise, is all the AI needs to proceed.

DOMAIN	ABILITIES	HIGH	STD	LOW
Physical	Fitness	☐	☐	☐
	Stamina	☐	☐	☐
	Strength	☐	☐	☐
	Recovery	☐	☐	☐
Emotional	Resilience	☐	☐	☐
	Stress Management	☐	☐	☐
	Emotional Balance	☐	☐	☐
	Moderation	☐	☐	☐
	Adaptability	☐	☐	☐
Cognitive	Problem-Solving	☐	☐	☐
	Analytical Thinking	☐	☐	☐
	Fast Learning	☐	☐	☐
	Memory	☐	☐	☐
	Creativity	☐	☐	☐
	Attention to Detail	☐	☐	☐
	Tolerance for Ambiguity	☐	☐	☐
	Hands-on	☐	☐	☐
Social	Expressiveness	☐	☐	☐
	Empathy	☐	☐	☐
	Outgoing	☐	☐	☐
	Good Communicator	☐	☐	☐
	Leadership Tendency	☐	☐	☐
	Teamwork	☐	☐	☐
Motivational	Confidence	☐	☐	☐
	Motivation	☐	☐	☐
	Assertiveness	☐	☐	☐
	Optimism	☐	☐	☐
	Initiative	☐	☐	☐
	Work Pace	☐	☐	☐
	Decisiveness	☐	☐	☐
Ethical	Responsibility	☐	☐	☐
	Reliability	☐	☐	☐
	Sense of Duty	☐	☐	☐

Fig. 38: Test your abilities (Appendix)

Remember that AI is only a tool. If you wish to receive professional advice, explore the options suggested in the last section of this chapter.

Lastly, prompts are as important as the information you provide to the AI. Suggestions for crafting more meaningful prompts are included in the Appendix, along with a full-page spreadsheet you can copy and use for the exercise.

Competency

We need skills but skills which fit our capacities. We could call it 'competency alignment.' This term suggests that a skill is not only appropriate but also well-suited to an individual's current abilities and potential for growth. We could just call it *competency*. Our competencies should align with specific roles or abilities that contribute to the overall goals, whether at work or within the family.

Outside the demands of an employment, *competency* can be a powerful tool for self-assessment, helping you identify your strengths, weaknesses, and areas for improvement. Self-assessment encourages critical thinking about personal abilities and fosters a drive for continuous improvement.

Aside from the professional or occupational skills, we need to work on other competencies like *family dynamics, communication, management,* and *digital proficiencies*. These skills are of great interest to boost self-confidence and add the touch we need to excel.

Family dynamics are the foundation of our interactions and personal development. They shape the essential skills needed to navigate and strengthen family relationships (i.e., spousal love, child-rearing, parental roles, authority and discipline). More than just communication, they set the tone for how we engage in both work and social settings; they influence every aspect of our life too.

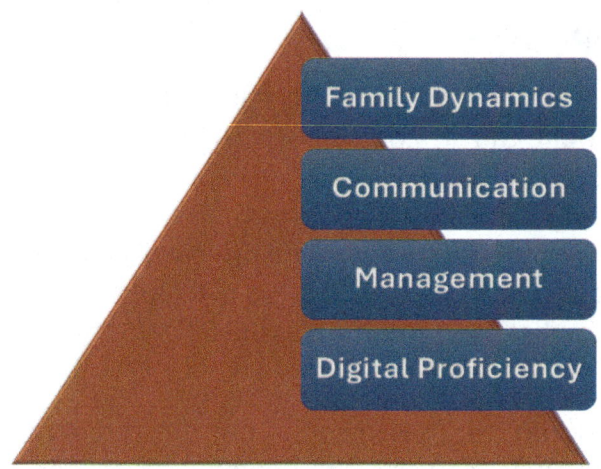

Fig. 39: Our competencies should align with the most common roles or abilities.

Communication is fundamental. We live and grow within a society, surrounded by people. Certain skills are essential to make progress, complete tasks, develop our thinking, earn respect by showing respect, foster a positive work environment, and maintain open channels of communication.

Management skills are complementary yet valuable too. Regardless of your responsibilities or position within the organizational structure, abilities such as time management, prioritization, goal setting, delegation, progress tracking, leadership (motivating and guiding a team), and conflict resolution can significantly impact your future success.

Today, *digital proficiency* is considered one of the most fundamental skills. It's often assumed rather than explicitly stated as a requirement, yet it's essential for both work and interpersonal interactions. Digital proficiency extends well beyond simply using a mobile phone; it includes the effective use of computers, communication devices, and other digital tools.

The main question is: how can I learn the skills I need, and how do I face the challenge?

Much can be said about this but perhaps not as much as the eccentric Elon Musk, who defends that conventional schooling can be overly rigid. Schools today fail to adapt to students' individual interests and aptitudes, which Elon believes should be central to education. According to Bloomberg's Billionaires Index, Elon Musk is generally regarded as one of the richest persons in the world, placing his net worth at about $251 billion[39]—which, let's face it, gives weight to his opinion and makes it relevant.

In 2014, Elon Musk co-founded a private school, Ad Astra, primarily for his children—today, Astra Nova. [40] At this school, Musk promoted hands-on problem-solving and avoided a conventional, grade-based curriculum. Instead, students learned by tackling real-world challenges. This method makes learning less tedious and more meaningful to students.

92—Capacity

His stance became more vocal by 2019, when he tweeted that 'formal degrees are not essential to work in my companies.' By 2020, He reiterated this sentiment during a 2020 Satellite Conference, declaring that college was 'for fun' and primarily served to test an individual's ability to complete tasks, rather than being a necessary step for gaining knowledge.

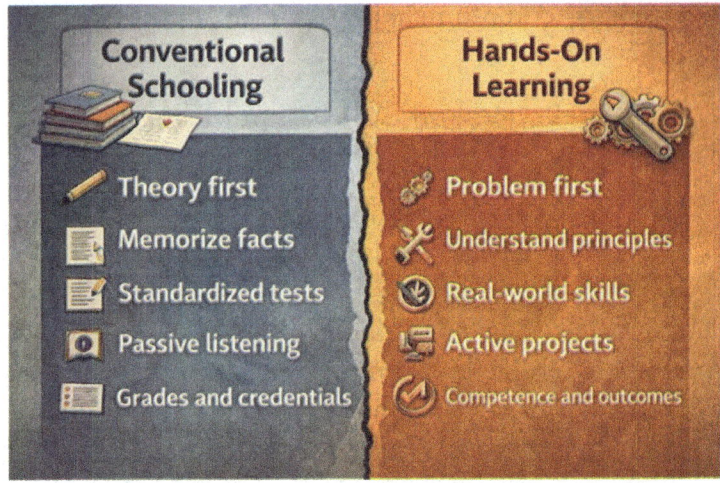

Fig. 40: Conventional Schooling vs. Hands-On Learning.

Since then, his critical views had become more radical, voicing admiration for skilled tradespeople, believing that practical, hands-on professions—like electricians or carpenters—can be more valuable than some academic degrees. In 2023,[41] Musk reiterated that a four-year college education is 'overrated' and that real-world experience and self-directed learning are often more effective. He argues that everything one needs to learn can be accessed independently.

He has a point. Certified online courses, YouTube videos, and Internet resources can help boost your knowledge and your skills—and even provide credentials. However, degrees are necessary in most parts of the world to apply for a job and grow in the professional ladder of the company you work for. Academic positions and government posts often require the highest educational achievements to land a top management job. But even in these cases the stand of Elon Musk makes sense because we often hear complaints about 'academicians' who know a lot about theories but little about the real world. To many, their 'overrated' knowledge is more of a hindrance than a benefit.

Based on the points discussed in this section, what would you consider your strengths and weaknesses? What do you believe you can achieve? Is there any other area of interest you'd like to explore further?

Avoid feeling overwhelmed by the task ahead. Filter your worries. Make a list of your strengths, followed by the skills that will help you develop them. Pairing your strengths with relevant skills will reveal your potential. However, you may need some guidance to identify your options. Lastly, explore online certifications and training resources to determine which ones can enhance your professional career or improve your job-related skills.

Though you might currently lack the time or resources, remember that the crucial element is your design—the blueprint of your resolve. Time will reveal its value. Take each step with patience and confidence in the direction you're shaping.

Self-Assessment

There are several self-tests and assessments available online that can help individuals evaluate their personal capacities and guide them toward improving their potential.

Currently, *StrengthsFinder* (from *CliftonStrengths*) is the most popular fee-based test designed to identify your top strengths, available through Gallup.[42] The *CliftonStrengths* assessment is the same one featured in *StrengthsFinder 2.0* and other bestselling books. Understanding your natural talents can help you focus on areas where you can excel and improve. The *VIA Character Strengths Survey*, offered by the VIA Institute, combines programmed and AI-assisted analysis to help individuals discover their core character strengths, which can be used to enhance healthy living and productivity.[43]

The well-known *Myers-Briggs Type Indicator* (MBTI) test helps individuals understand their personality types—MBTI assessment identifies 16 distinct personality types. "Each type reflects how a person naturally prefers to direct and receive energy, take in information, make decisions, and approach the outside world. Knowing this provides a powerful framework for understanding and relating to people."[44] Variations of personality tests, like the one offered for free by *InsightfulTraits* [45] and Mindmetrics [46] —AI powered—are also available.

These tests can help individuals leverage their strengths, collaborate effectively with others, and identify areas for personal improvement.

The newly coined Emotional Intelligence (EI) is a basic component of personal growth, effective leadership, and meaningful relationships. There are several tests available online to assist with your personal inquiries. The Personality Lab offers you the option to find you Emotional Quotient (EQ) through a 'Research-based Emotional Intelligence Test.'[47] The rather complicated, and expensive, "EQ-i 2.0 test is one of the most scientifically validated Emotional Intelligence instruments on the market today."[48] This instrument measures the interaction between a person and his or her environment that can help assess your emotional intelligence and suggest areas for improvement. "The EQ-i 2.0 model shows how five Composite Scales and fifteen Subscales interact to predict behaviors. The circular nature of the model is a visual representation of how each area of Emotional Intelligence influences the next."[49]

Other models focus on evaluating specific aspects of an individual's personality to help improve targeted areas of development.

The *Big Five Personality Test* is another application popularized by *The Personality Lab*.[50] This is a psychological model for understanding personality. It evaluates individuals based on five major traits: openness, conscientiousness, extraversion, agreeableness, and neuroticism.

The *Self-Compassion Scale* focuses on building emotional resilience. A single one-page questionary[51] will measure how kindly you treat yourself during moments of failure or difficulty.

Fig. 41: Self-assessment test.

The *Grit Scale Test* by the psychologist Angela Duckworth measures your level of perseverance and passion for long-term goals. Another one-page questioner that ends with "a score that reflects how passionate and persevering you see yourself to be."[52] It's a good indicator of personal resilience and determination.

The free or paid versions of these tests are valuable tools for self-reflection and for improving aspects of your personal and professional life that may often be hidden from view. Tests offered by well-known companies are often expensive, but the decision to take one depends on the personal evaluation of your needs. Before committing to a fee-based test, it's wise to conduct further research to assess its reliability and effectiveness.

Conclusion

I know what you are thinking: 'This is too much for me. So many things to work on! So many question marks and uncertainties!' You don't need to work on every aspect of life management at one point. Actually, you shouldn't. You only need a start and perhaps a strategy.

Fig. 42: A Personal Life Project.

Take it one step at a time. Start by following the priorities outlined in the first area of interest, *Context*. Then, work on recording your monthly income and expenses to assess your financial power. Next, project your expenses into the future, aligning them with your short- and long-term goals, to determine what your target income should be. Finally, consider what type of professional development would best support your abilities and the plan that you are outlining.

What strategy can ensure the success of a life management project? We could extract several very interesting recommendations from experts in parallel fields who wrote about personal projects as well.[53]

1. Every life project is *personal* and should be treated as such. It should reflect the type of person I am because I am the protagonist.

2. A life project should follow some *basic orderly structure* to avoid deviations and random improvisation. Order within a well-thought system is always advantageous and facilitates consistency.

3. My objectives should be *realistic* and, in a way, demanding. If my life project is designed based on concrete realistic objectives, they are attainable.

4. I should not forget that every personal project requires *effort*. Effort is manifested through a firm desire to achieve an objective and a determined disposition to fight laziness, comfort-seeking, and to overcome routine.

5. A personal project requires a certain *inner strength* that we might not initially possess, but which can be developed along the way. It demands focusing and the fortitude of saying no to variations which can take us away from our true goal and purpose.

6. Lastly, due to the complexity of life and our inherent condition as humans, which makes us prone to failure, we will often need to *realign and retrace* our itinerary.

Tex

Appendix

We can break down the list of personal capacities or domains—presented in the section titled "What are you good at?" in Chapter Seven—into a spreadsheet of thirty-three common abilities relevant to our work and lifestyle. The list could easily be expanded, so this selection focuses on the most representative abilities within each domain.

These six domains will help us identify what we are good at and what we may be missing. However, it is difficult to reach any meaningful conclusion without some form of external support.

Today, we are fortunate to rely on a highly versatile tool: Artificial Intelligence, which searches the Internet for answers, analyzes the results, and presents them in formats that are easy to understand and assimilate. AI can be consulted through prompts and uploads.

To reach meaningful conclusions from the attached spreadsheet, print a copy and mark each ability as HIGH, STD, or LOW—according to your personal interpretation of character and personality. Finally, take a picture of your completed sheet with your mobile phone and upload it to your preferred AI engine.

Please remember that the information provided by AI should always be verified, and the results of this exercise are for informational purposes only.

If you need professional advice, there are self-tests and assessments available online, ranging from free to paid versions.

Consider the following general prompt to accompany your upload:

"Here are my ability ratings (HIGH / STD / LOW). Please analyze them and give me:

- my main strengths,
- areas for improvement,
- my general temperament style (non-clinical),
- the types of work or environments I may thrive in,
- any patterns or tendencies worth noting."

If you need more information on specific areas, AI may suggest using a more detailed prompt that describes the context and the depth of the answers you require. You can even ask AI to provide prompt options similar to the ones listed below.

"Based on my ratings (HIGH / STD / LOW), analyze the patterns you see in my abilities. Identify my strongest domains, my average areas, and the abilities I may want to improve."

"Describe my general temperament style based on these abilities, using non-clinical language."

"Given my ability ratings, what types of work environments, roles, or tasks am I likely to perform well in? Please explain why these fit my strengths."

DOMAIN	ABILITIES	HIGH	STD	LOW
Physical	Fitness	☐	☐	☐
Physical	Stamina	☐	☐	☐
Physical	Strength	☐	☐	☐
Physical	Recovery	☐	☐	☐
Emotional	Resiliance	☐	☐	☐
Emotional	Stress Management	☐	☐	☐
Emotional	Emotional Balance	☐	☐	☐
Emotional	Moderation	☐	☐	☐
Emotional	Adaptability	☐	☐	☐
Cognitive	Problem-Solving	☐	☐	☐
Cognitive	Analytical Thinking	☐	☐	☐
Cognitive	Fast Learning	☐	☐	☐
Cognitive	Memory	☐	☐	☐
Cognitive	Creativity	☐	☐	☐
Cognitive	Attention to Detail	☐	☐	☐
Cognitive	Tolerance for Ambiguit	☐	☐	☐
Cognitive	Hands-on	☐	☐	☐
Social	Expressiveness	☐	☐	☐
Social	Empathy	☐	☐	☐
Social	Outgoing	☐	☐	☐
Social	Good Communicator	☐	☐	☐
Social	Leadership Tendency	☐	☐	☐
Social	Teamwork	☐	☐	☐
Motivational	Confidence	☐	☐	☐
Motivational	Motivation	☐	☐	☐
Motivational	Assertiveness	☐	☐	☐
Motivational	Optimism	☐	☐	☐
Motivational	Initiative	☐	☐	☐
Motivational	Work Pace	☐	☐	☐
Motivational	Decisiveness	☐	☐	☐
Ethical	Responsibiliy	☐	☐	☐
Ethical	Reliability	☐	☐	☐
Ethical	Sense of Duty	☐	☐	☐

About the Author

The author–by the nickname of Tex, obtained a Licentiate in Biology with a specialization in Zoology from the State University of Valencia, Spain. He also completed a Certificate in Education at the University of Alicante, which qualified him for teaching positions. Additionally, he holds a Diploma in Affectivity and Sexuality from the University of Navarre in Spain.

In the Philippines he ventured into other fields to add to his humanistic and technical formation finishing a master's in library and information sciences by the University of the Philippines in Diliman, that he completed with a subspecialty in library software and history and the publication of articles in specialized journals together with the printing of the book *History of Books and Libraries in the Philippines, 1521-1900*. He has also published software for library management.

He has occupied management positions in cultural centers, lectured extensively about value education, engaged in school consultancies, mentoring, and counseling. He is an avid cyclist and motorist and has been everywhere North to South in the Philippines.

Other Works by the Author

Tex Hernandez is the author of several thought-provoking books that explore some of life's biggest questions—touching on values like personal growth, relationships, identity, and decision-making. His works are brought together under the engaging umbrella of *The Big-Question Series*, with each title offering a fresh take on challenges we all face.

Am I an Atheist? Science, Atheism, and the Way of Friendship – A thoughtful look at the relationship between science and belief, and how both shape the way we connect with others.

Should I Marry? The Essential Guide to Discernment – A guide to understanding what makes commitment meaningful and how it relates to happiness and lasting success.

Shall I Dress It? Sexuality in Overdrive – An eye-opening examination of the powerful pull of sexuality, including perspectives on addiction and identity.

What Are My Chances? Life Management Explained – A practical and inspiring guide to navigating life's choices and finding a sense of purpose through planning.

Why Character? The Quest That Matters – The newest addition, offering fresh insights into character development through five essential pillars.

All titles in *The Big-Question Series* are available online via Google Play Books and Amazon Kindle.

Notes

¹ Wikipedia, 'The Shape of My Heart (Sting Song),' September 21, 2024 (wikipedia.org).

² Viktor E. Frankl, Man's Search for Meaning (London: Rider, 2004), p. 21.

³ Here, I dare to quote my own published words from Chapter Four, in the section on "Right and Wrong," of my book Why Character (available online through Google Play Books and Amazon Kindle, in both electronic and printed formats).

⁴ Enrique Rojas, Remedios para el Desamor, pp. 45 & 54.

⁵ Repeat-Replay, 'What Percent of Song are about Love,' 2024 (https://repeatreplay.com/what-percent-of-songs-are-about-love/?form=MG0AV3).

⁶ Dietrich von Hildebrand, Man and Woman (Manchester, New Hampshire: Sophia Institute Press, 1992), 'The Nature of Love,' p. 10.

⁷ Cormac Burke, Covenanted Happiness, Third Edition (The United Kingdom: The Dunstan Trust, 2019), 'What Marriage is for,' p. 55.

⁸ The subject under scrutiny—love—has led me to revisit and echo some ideas I explored earlier in my book Should I Marry?. If you haven't read that book, you may find these ideas fresh; otherwise, they may feel familiar.

⁹ Marie Claire, '8 Quotes That Prove Jennifer Lopez Is The Queen Of Body Confidence,' 2015 (https://www.marieclaire.co.uk/news/beauty-news/jennifer-lopez-body-quotes-118759?form=MG0AV3).

¹⁰ Kendra Cherry, MSEd, 'Loneliness: Causes and Health Consequences,' December 5, 2023

(https://www.verywellmind.com/loneliness-causes-effects-and-treatments-2795749).

[11] Enrique Rojas, *Remedios para el Desamor, Como Afrontar las Crisis de la Pareja* (Madrid: Planeta, 1999), p. 84.

[12] Located in a cave site in Morocco, these fossils were first discovered in the 1960s. Initially thought to be around 40,000 years old, 2017 research utilized thermoluminescence dating to reveal they are approximately 315,000 years old (See Wikipedia, 'Jebel Irhoud').

[13] 'Oldest Human Remains in the World,' 2025 (https://www.oldest.org/people/human-remains/)

[14] Our Norwegian protagonist, Roald Amundsen (1872-1928) is, perhaps, one of the greatest explorers of all time. He was a man of science, courage, and honor, a true friend to his friends who died in a futile attempt to rescue his friend Umberto Moville. His body was never found. You can read a summary of his achievements in the Wikipedia but his biographer, Roland Huntford, a British historian, offers a much more detailed and enticing reading. Huntford's *The Last Place on Earth* focuses on the expeditions of Amundsen and Robert Falcon Scott (1868-1912) as they competed to reach the South Pole in 1911.

[15] In the South Pole, at an altitude of approximately 2,835 meters (9,301 feet) above sea level, an extreme drop of temperature can cause the rapid freezing of water. Robert Scott and his team were exposed to extreme cold, exhaustion, and malnutrition; a severe blizzard could have brought about the sudden death of the team. Scott's last diary entry was on March 29, 1912. Their bodies were found in their tent eight months later.

[16] Worldometers, 'Life Expectancy of the World Population,' 2024, based on the latest *United Nations Population Division* estimates (worldometers.info/demographics/life-expectancy/).

[17] Peter W. Frank and Lawrence Kaplan, 'Human Life Span,' Britannica online, October 11, 2024 (britannica.com/science/).

[18] Patrick Aubert, 'Age, wage and productivity: firm-level evidence,' December 2006 (researchgate.net/publication/228600663).

[19] Copilot, Responses to Productivity in relation to age,' November 2, 2024 (https://time.thecommonvein.net/productivity/).

[20] *My Life as an Explorer* by Roald Amundsen (London: Heinemann, 1927).

[21] *Roald Amundsen* by Tor Bomann-Larsen (Sutton, 2006).

[22] https://www.redbull.com/ph-en/alex-honnold-life-after-free-solo.

[23] Carlos Beltramo, "Cinco pilares del carácter y apertura a la trascendencia," In M. L. Diez Canseco Briceño (Ed.), *Actas del seminario, Psicología desde una visión cristiana del hombre* (pp. 7–18) (Arequipa, Perú: Universidad Católica San Pablo, 2023) (https://ucsp.edu.pe/actas-seminario-psicologia-desde-vision-cristiana-hombre/).

[24] Both books—*Why Character?* and *What Are My Chances?*—originally appeared together in a single volume titled *Life Management* as part of *The Big-Question Series*. I may eventually reintegrate them, but the decision to separate them was purely practical. Completing one book at a time makes the material easier to absorb and prevents the heaviness of a thick, consolidated volume.

[25] Jennifer Herrity, 'What is Management?', October 16, 2024, *Indeed Career Guide* (https://www.indeed.com/career-advice/career-development/).

[26] Enrique Rojas, *Remedios para el Desamor* (Madrid: Planeta, 2003), p. 10.

[27] Diosdado Marasigan, 'Foreword,' in Mina, Achilles, Editor in Chief, *The Educhild Story, From Playgrounds to Promising Futures* (Manila: Media Wise Communications, Inc./ Muse Books, 2023).

[28] Kevin Benneth, *10 Good Reasons to Keep a Diary*, Psychology Today, January 31, 2023 (https://www.psychologytoday.com/us/blog/modern-minds/202301/10-good-reasons-to-keep-a-journal).

[29] *Ibid.*

[30] There are countless online sources offering advice on investment and job opportunities. Perhaps the two following websites summarize, to some extent, the possibilities available in today's job market. Manish Sahajwani , '6 Best Paying Jobs in Finance,' October 18, 2024 (www.investopedia.com/financial-edge/0112), and Grit PH, '12 Profitable Side Hustles for Filipinos in 2024,' September 3, 2024 (https://grit.ph/side-hustle/?form=MG0AV3).

[31] Tex Hernandez, *Should I Marry?* (Manila: Self-Published, 2024), Chapter 5.

[32] The United Nations has documented that there are around 1.6 billion people residing in poor housing worldwide, with around 15 million being forcibly evicted each year. Surprisingly, living in a rich country or healthy economy is no guarantee of being "homelessness immune." (Daniil Filipenco, 'Homelessness statistics in the world: causes and facts,' December 13, 2023, [https://www.developmentaid.org/news-stream/post/157797/]).

[33] In a ChatGPT conversation on 'Personal Finances' (Nov 8, 2024), the following sources provide detailed advice for budgeting and managing debt effectively, grounded in widely recognized financial principles: the Consumer Financial Protection Bureau (CFPB) (www.consumerfinance.gov), the Federal Trade Commission (FTC) (www.ftc.gov), Dave Ramsey's Financial Advice (www.ramseysolutions.com), National Foundation for Credit Counseling (NFCC)

(www.nfcc.org), NerdWallet and Investopedia (www.nerdwallet.com, www.investopedia.com).

[34] Steve Martin, Bill Hader, and Kristen Wiig, 'Don't Buy Stuff - Saturday Night Live,' September 1, 2013, 0:02:47 (https://youtu.be/R3ZJKN_5M44?si=wSdYg6WkWiVg_kg-).

[35] Xin Lu, 'Chinese Money Habits - How My Culture Influences My Attitudes Toward Money,' Wisebread, 2024 (wisebread.com).

[36] These are widely accepted personal finance principles and best practices shared by *Your Money or Your Life* by Vicki Robin and Joe Dominguez, the National Endowment for Financial Education (NEFE), and Fidelity and Vanguard Investment Guides.

[37] Certain types of insurance can indeed help reduce your tax burden by offering tax deductions, exemptions, or other benefits. A few examples are Life Insurances, Health Savings Accounts (HAS), Long-Term Care Insurances, Disability Insurances, and Retirement-Linked Insurances. Tax advantages vary by country and policy. It is therefore a good idea to consult a tax professional or financial advisor.

[38] Microsoft 365, 'Personal budgeting templates for achieving your financial goals,' 2025 (https://create.microsoft.com/en-us/templates/personal-budgeting).

[39] Forbes, 'The Top 10 Richest People in the World,' October 2024 (https://www.forbes.com.au/news/billionaires/who-are-the-10-richest-people-in-the-world/).

[40] Wikipedia, 'Astra Nova School,' October 26, 2024 (https://en.m.wikipedia.org/wiki/Astra_Nova_School).

[41] Elon Musk, 'You don't need a college degree,' YouTube video, 0:08:11, January 9, 2023 (https://www.youtube.com/watch%3Fv).

[42] Gallup, 'Looking for StrengthsFinder? You're in the right place,' 2025 (https://www.gallup.com/cliftonstrengths/en/254033/strengthsfinder.aspx).

[43] VIA Institute on Character, 'Who are you at your best?' 2025 (https://www.viacharacter.org/).

[44] The Myers-Briggs Company, 'Self-awareness starts here,' 2025 (https://www.themyersbriggs.com/en-US/Products-and-Services/Myers-Briggs).

[45] InsightfulTraits, 'Free Personality Test,' 2025 (https://insightfultraits.com/lp/freepersonalitytest/).

[46] Mindmetrics.ai, 'Discover the Depth of Your Personality!' 2025 (https://mindmetric.ai/personality?gad_source).

[47] The Personality Lab, 'Research-based Emotional Intelligence Test,' 2025 (https://www.thepersonalitylab.org/eq-test?gad_source).

[48] High Performing Systems, Inc., 'EQ-i$^{2.0}$,' 2025 (https://www.hpsys.com/EI_EQ-i2.0Home.htm).

[49] *Ibid.*

[50] The Personality Lab, 'With the BIG 5 personality test, you will find out what personality type you are,' 2025 (https://www.thepersonalitylab.org/big5?gad_source).

[51] Kristin Neff, 'Self-Compassion,' 2024 (self-compassion.org/self-compassion-test/).

[52] Angela Duckworth, 'Grit Scale,' 2025 (https://angeladuckworth.com/grit-scale/).

[53] Enrique Rojas, *Remedios para el Desamor*, pp. 41-43.

Made in the USA
Coppell, TX
28 February 2026

72589568R00069